BE A YOUNG
ENTREPRENEUR

WRITTEN BY
ADAM SUTHERLAND

ILLUSTRATED BY
MIKE GORDON

WAYLAND

Published in Great Britain in 2018 by Wayland

Text © Wayland, 2016
Illustration © Mike Gordon, 2016
Written by Adam Sutherland

Editor: Corinne Lucas
Designer: Alyssa Peacock

ISBN 978 0 7502 9835 3
10 9

Wayland, an imprint of Hachette Children's Group. Part of Hodder & Stoughton
Carmelite House, 50 Victoria Embankment, London, EC4Y 0DZ

An Hachette UK Company
www.hachette.co.uk
www.hachettechildrens.co.uk

Printed in Dubai

CONTENTS

WHY BE A YOUNG ENTREPRENEUR?

DO YOU WANT TO:

* work for yourself
* do something you enjoy
* use your imagination
* meet new people
* learn new skills
* make some money?

OF COURSE YOU DO!

Starting your own business is exciting and rewarding, but it can also be complicated and scary at times. Don't worry, *Be a Young Entrepreneur* will take you step by step through everything you need to know — from what kind of business you should choose, through researching the market, writing a business plan, choosing — and registering — a company name and website address, telling people about your business (that's called marketing, in entrepreneur-speak), and looking after your finances.

Notes

YOU'LL ALSO READ:

1 inspirational stories of other young entrepreneurs — and how they achieved success

2 examples from the experts — famous companies who have become household names

3 tips on building a successful brand

4 advice on earning money — and keeping it.

So what are you waiting for? Let's get started!

CHAPTER 1: TIME TO MAKE PLANS

"If you're really interested in something, go with it and don't be afraid to take risks. Being an entrepreneur is all about taking risks."

Zach Weisenthal (ZacksWebDesigns.com)

5 GREAT REASONS TO BE AN ENTREPRENEUR

Starting a business can be hard and take up a lot of time — time that could be spent seeing friends, watching TV … even doing homework! Sometimes you might wish you hadn't even started. To stay motivated, here are five reasons to begin your own business.

1 YOU'LL BECOME MORE CONFIDENT

You'll be starting a business from nothing, learning everything you can about running it, contacting people you've never met, possibly even standing in front of people and 'pitching' your services. How can you not be more confident after all that!

2 YOU'LL MAKE NEW FRIENDS

We can guarantee you one thing — 12 months after you start your own business, you'll know loads more people than you do today. You'll meet local businesses that you sell to, and customers who hire you. You'll meet other young people who are starting businesses and spend time swapping stories, and giving and receiving advice.

3 YOU'LL GET REALLY GOOD AT SOMETHING

Whatever business you start, stick with it and you'll become an expert at it. Trust us, you may think you're good now, but hours and hours spent on the job, facing problems and solving them will make you a virtual gold medal winner in your chosen business.

BUSINESS TIP
When you're polishing that gold medal, take any opportunity to lend your expert opinions to magazine articles, web interviews and so on. It's great advertising for you and your business.

4 YOU CAN BE CREATIVE

Creativity isn't just about being good at drawing or making Origami cranes — it's about being able to dream up new business ideas, working out how to make progress with your business, finding new areas to grow into, launching new products and services ... in fact, anything you can cook up in that big entrepreneurial brain of yours. So get your thinking cap on.

5 YOU CAN MAKE SOME MONEY

Oh yes, did we mention that people actually pay you for having all this fun? Some successful entrepreneurs make millions of pounds and become world famous! Our tip for success: concentrate on providing the very best product or service you can, and treat your customers with respect. Who knows, you might end up buying your own island one day like Richard Branson.

10 BUSINESS IDEAS FOR KIDS

OK, you've been inspired by our five great reasons to start a business, and you want to have a go yourself. The next step is to think hard about what kind of business you will start.

The key to a successful business is to find a need, fill it and monetise (in other words, make money from) the service. Think about not only what you're good at and what interests you, but also what people might want or need. Maybe you already know what sort of business you will start. But if you don't, read on for inspiration.

1 TECH GURU

All kids know that grown-ups can barely operate a TV remote control, let alone store their mobile phone pictures to the Cloud. But you can! So why not advertise your tech problem-solving services to the local community: smartphones set up, emails synced, Wi-Fi networks joined — and even Smart TVs programmed. Not to mention backing up photos and data on the Cloud or similar remote services. You might even want to teach mum and dad a thing or two — if they can afford you.

If you press here it turns the camera around and you can take a selfie.

2 YOUTUBER

3 APP BUILDER

Lots of young people are building huge followings — and making good incomes — from their YouTube channels. Whether you want to give make-up and fashion advice like Zoella, play video games like KSI, or something entirely different, there's a channel for you. If you're thinking of becoming a YouTuber, read up on how to create watchable videos. As your channel grows, you can earn money from subscriptions, but also from brands who will pay to have their new products promoted on popular channels.

Experts think the mobile apps market is worth over £95 billion per year worldwide — and it's still growing. Apps don't have to be complicated to be successful — often it's the opposite. Think how addictive Candy Crush or Angry Birds are. If you're seriously considering app building as your start-up business, you'll need a decent understanding of coding and a clear plan of what you want to achieve and how.

YOUNG ENTREPRENEUR: EVANTUBEHD

The secret of business? Do what you love and get paid for it! Toy and game fan Evan started reviewing toys and building Lego online at the age of five. Now, the nine year old has over 2.5 million subscribers on YouTube and his videos have been watched over one billion times! www.youtube.com/user/EvanTubeHD

A COUPLE OF USEFUL ARTICLES HERE:

http://experts.allbusiness.com/12-step-guide-to-building-your-first-mobile-app/11193/#.VajfTWC5f0d

http://www.forbes.com/sites/allbusiness/2013/11/14/how-to-build-your-first-mobile-app-in-12-steps-part-2/

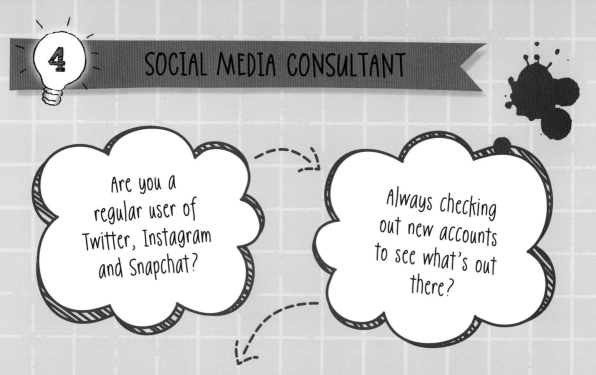

Are you a regular user of Twitter, Instagram and Snapchat?

Always checking out new accounts to see what's out there?

Consider putting that social media expertise to good use as a social media consultant. What comes easily to you, could be extremely valuable to companies and brands. Think about businesses in your area — they could be a coffee shop, a baker, a florist or whatever. How could they let more potential customers know about what services they offer, and how good they are? We suggest putting together a simple sales pitch that describes what you do, and how you can help them. Think about how long it will take you, and what you will charge. This sort of business can quickly spread by word of mouth, and you could have other interested businesses contacting you for your services in no time.

You need a blooming good website!

If you enjoy writing, and have a passion for fashion — or food, football, or anything else for that matter — why not set up your own blog? In 2003, Martin Lewis started his MoneySavingExpert.com blog. Nine years later he sold it to Moneysupermarket.com for a whopping £87 million. The majority of bloggers don't become multimillionaires, but most do earn money from their efforts through something called 'affiliate marketing'. Put simply, these are banner ads on your pages. If someone clicks on one of these, and ends up making a purchase, you'll make a percentage of the money, usually between 5–15 per cent. Industry experts estimate that the average fashion or beauty blogger earns around £1,000 per year from

their site from 'click-throughs'. Another way to make money from your blog — similar to YouTube — is to get paid by brands who sponsor you. If you're a food blogger, for example, you might be sponsored by a brand of flour, or a specific store, to mention it in your recipes. Don't forget fast-growing social media routes like Snapchat and Vine, they're also great platforms for promotion and will only get bigger.

Make sure the box doesn't cover my face.

6 EBAY SELLER

Who doesn't have LOADS of useless stuff kicking around the house that they don't want? Not only could you get rid of your old clothes, games, and so on, and make some extra cash, but once you've learned the ropes you could be selling stuff for friends, family or whoever – for a share of the profits, of course! Read up on how to set up a seller account (you might need a parent's help, depending on your age) on sites such as Gumtree, eBay and Preloved, and start small. Research the cost of similar items online – is yours in better condition? Worse? Don't forget to factor in postal costs – for the envelopes, as well as the stamps – or you could see your profits quickly disappear at the Post Office. Once you've run out of things to sell at home, design some flyers and put them through your neighbours' letterboxes. You could be bringing in regular income from your bedroom with no costs, and a minimal investment of time.

7 WEB DESIGNER

We don't recommend this one unless you have some experience of design and/or building and maintaining your own website. You do? Well this could be for you. WordPress is the most popular site-building platform out there – it's easy to use, free (yes, free), and simple to change once it's up. There are also loads of really useful tutorials available online so you can keep learning. There's some great info here:

✳ http://www.creativebloq.com/web-design/wordpress-tutorials-designers-1012990

Take our advice and learn everything you can about the nuts and bolts of building a site, then go out and sell yourself to clients. For most people, building their own website seems as complicated as constructing a rocket to the moon. If your designs are good and your work professional, you could be getting lots of bookings from local businesses and beyond in no time.

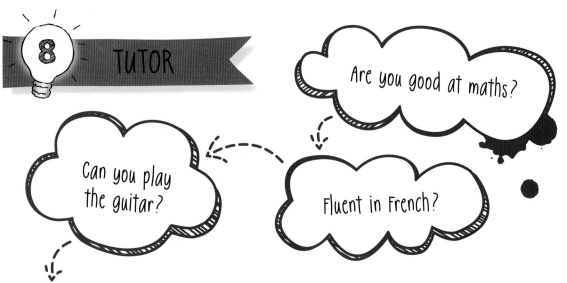

The chances are there's something you're very good at that you could teach to someone else. Whatever you decide to teach, we suggest picking a younger age group to teach it to. You'll need to think about what you will charge per hour or half hour, and whether to charge for materials on top, for example text books or revision guides. Just as important, you should plan not only your first lesson but also a series of lessons from the start. That way, you can work out how you get from A to Z in the simplest and most understandable way. In other words, if you're teaching guitar, teach the basic chord structures first before you try and turn your pupil into a rock god!

GIFT MAKER AND SELLER

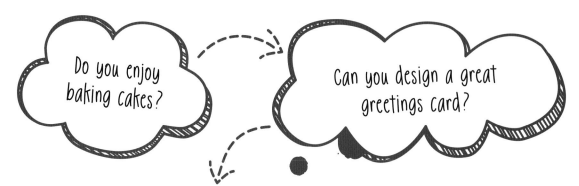

Do you enjoy baking cakes?

Can you design a great greetings card?

Why not put your creativity to the test by making and selling to local shops or online via eBay, or specialist gift sites like www.notonthehighstreet.com. It pays to do your homework first: visit local retailers who sell the sort of thing you're planning to make.

Who's their current supplier? How much do they pay per item? You'll need all this information to work out your price point and your profit margin (see Chapter 5). Fingers crossed, you'll soon be doing something that you enjoy and making money from it!

Research is my favourite part of my cake business!

If you're a pet lover, this is just the job for you! Most pet owners would prefer to leave their furry friends at home when they go on holiday than put them in a kennel or cattery. The much-loved family pet would be far happier cuddled up on a favourite chair. So why not advertise your services as a pet sitter? Your neighbours will know you, and be more comfortable giving you the keys to their house than a stranger. Treat it like your own place (we don't mean leave dirty socks behind the TV) — keep everything tidy, and lock the doors behind you when you leave.

Dog walking is another great money-earner. Dog owners who work long hours are often looking for someone to take Fido for a run around the park to burn off some energy during the day. Remember to keep dogs on a lead unless told otherwise, and yes you do have to scoop the poop. Sorry, that's part of the job!

10 TOUGH QUESTIONS

You've chosen your business, and you're ready to go. Oh no, you're not. Not until you've answered our 10 tough questions. Notebook and pen at the ready! Put some thought into these and give yourself a head start.

1 DO YOU HAVE THE TIME TO START A BUSINESS?

You're at school all day, so your business will have to fit around the spare time you have after school, during weekends and holidays. Bear that in mind when you're choosing your business. Whether you want to bake cakes or fix computers, work out how many spare hours you can dedicate to it, and plan from there.

YOUNG ENTREPRENEUR: ZOLLIPOPS

Zollipops are sugar-free lollipops from nine-year-old entrepreneur Alina Morse. They taste good and the ingredients help neutralise acidity in the mouth and prevent tooth decay! Alina has been on the kids' version of 'Shark Tank', the US version of 'Dragon's Den'. www.zollipops.com

2 HAVE YOU RESEARCHED THE MARKET?

Who else is out there doing what you want to do? Loads of people? Mmm, perhaps think of another idea unless you really think you can offer something better. If there are no other businesses offering what you do, find out why. Have they closed down? If you have found a new area, congratulations!

3 WHAT ARE YOUR USPs?

Every business needs some USPs. That's 'Unique Selling Points' to you and me: reasons why customers buy from one company, or one product, and not from the competition. If you're offering guitar lessons, why not offer 'Play your favourite song in four weeks or your money back'?

GREAT EXAMPLES OF COMPANY USPs

To fly, to save
Easyjet

When it absolutely, positively
has to be there overnight
FedEx®

Eat Fresh®
Subway®

The milk chocolate melts in
your mouth, not in your hand™
M&Ms®

Pizza delivered in 30
minutes or it's free
Dominos Pizza®

4 DO PEOPLE WANT IT?

How do you know there are potential customers out there who want what you're selling? Simple, ask them! We recommend writing down a short list of questions (so you remember them) and then asking friends, neighbours, local businesses or doing an online survey (see page 42). Ask whoever is appropriate for the kind of business you want to start. Try and talk to as many people as you can. That way, you'll start to see some points appearing regularly, and those are the ones to take special notice of.

5 WHAT'S YOUR BUSINESS MODEL?

Relax, this is just a business-y way of asking how much will you charge people, and what will you charge them for. Will you be making something? In which case your price will need to include your own costs (to buy materials and so on). Or will you be offering a service, like repairing someone's computer, in which case you're charging for your time plus possibly some travel costs to get to and from the customer?

6   IS THE PRICE RIGHT?

It's important to make sure your business is 'competitively priced'. In other words, a) can people afford it, and b) is it worth what you are charging? You need to answer 'yes' to a) and b). If possible, research the pricing of similar businesses. You could also talk to potential customers (see point 4) and ask them what they would be prepared to pay.

7   CAN YOU MAKE A PROFIT?

You're going to be working hard, and although you'll also be having fun, it's important that you earn money. This links to point 6 above – if it costs you £2 to make a cake, don't sell it for £1.50. If you need to spend £50 on revision guides to teach French, how many lessons will you have to book to make that money back? Finances are a vitally important part of your business. For more details, turn to Chapter 5.

8   DO YOU HAVE ENOUGH MONEY TO GET STARTED?

Big businesses cost thousands, sometimes millions, of pounds to set up. Luckily, you are starting small and growing from there. Your business might need anything from £10–100 to get started. Whatever the case, do you have the money yourself? Will you borrow it from someone? If so, make sure you pay it back.

OK, let me check under the sofa cushions...

9 CAN THE BUSINESS GROW?

You might not be thinking about it now, but the business that you start today could be around for many years to come. Consider how you could expand it in the future: would you employ more staff? Rent a commercial kitchen to bake bigger and better cakes? The sky is the limit if you get the basics right!

10 DO YOU HAVE WHAT IT TAKES TO MAKE IT WORK?

All entrepreneurs – young or old – need a range of skills that will help them succeed.

CREATIVITY
You need to be good at coming up with new ideas and strategies to move your business forward.

ENTHUSIASM
Believe in what you're selling, and others will too!

OPTIMISM
From time to time things won't go according to plan. When things go wrong it's important to pick yourself back up and keep trying.

MAKING DECISIONS
New businesses require hundreds of decisions, from colours to flavours, sizes to prices. Can you make them, and be confident in your instincts and research?

HARD WORKING
Once you start attracting customers, you'll get busy. Are you prepared to spend the time you need to on your business? If you'd prefer chatting with friends to meeting clients and fulfilling orders, think again before you get started.

GOOD COMMUNICATOR
Can you answer questions about your business knowledgeably? Write, send emails and make phone calls confidently and clearly?

CHAPTER 2:
WHAT BUSINESS IS RIGHT FOR YOU?

"It's okay to fail the first time. You can try again with a fresh idea."

Ed Hardy (co-creator of Edge app)

LET'S GET STARTED

You've asked yourself our 10 Tough Questions, and you think you've got a great business idea. Hooray! No one can guarantee your business will make it big, but if we have one tip for success, it's **forward planning**. From understanding your market to writing a business plan, we're with you every step of the way.

GETTING TO KNOW YOUR MARKET

Stop and think … it's important not to rush into business without doing everything you can to check that your idea fits into the market. Whatever your idea, your aim is the same — to stand out. And your most important tool for that is market research.

What similar businesses are already out there?

What do they do differently from you, and from each other?

What customers use each business (and, if possible, why)?

20

YOUNG ENTREPRENEUR: NOT BEFORE TEA

Eleven-year-old Henry Patterson from Bedfordshire, England is the founder of 'children's lifestyle brand' Not Before Tea. The company started life as an online sweet shop, and has now grown to include books and merchandise. Henry first went into business at age seven, selling bags of manure for £1 each! www.notbeforetea.co.uk

WHY IT'S IMPORTANT

A better understanding of the market and how the competition does business, will help you create a good business strategy. Will you be aiming at 100 or 1,000 customers? What can you offer that they don't? The more information you can get and problems you can spot early on, means the less time and money you will waste later.

Good news: you don't need a team of highly paid market researchers. You can do it all yourself with a computer, a travel pass, some paper and a pen. Here's how.

ONLINE

Make a list of keywords you would use to advertise your own business online – things like 'computer repairs', 'technical support' and so on. Then do a web search of businesses offering the same thing in your area. If you find a direct competitor (someone offering the same product or service as you), have a look at their website – how do they promote themselves? What age group are they appealing to?

If there's no competition, or if people have tried it already and failed, that's something you can find out in face-to-face questions.

Check with the Office for National Statistics (*http://www.ons.gov.uk/ons/index.html*). You might want to research how many over-50-year-olds are using smartphones, for example, to see the size of your market.

You Gov Reports (*https://yougov. co.uk/find-solutions/ reports/*) might look tricky, but browsing a few reports could give you some ideas to help you tweak your plans.

I've just sold Harold's walking stick on eBay.

FACE TO FACE

Here's where you need the travel pass, paper and pen. Write a list of simple questions (and space for answers), and head for the high street. Don't just do it once, go back a few times at different times and on different days. That way you should get a wider range of people for your research.

Your questions will obviously depend on what sort of business you want to launch, but try and include a question on pricing. For example, 'How much would you be prepared to pay for this service or product?' You could also suggest a range of prices if you're not sure what to charge. Ask people politely if they mind answering a few questions. You'll get some people refusing but hopefully some will agree – and some of those people may be happy to talk in more detail. Listen to what they've got to say – it could be useful!

BE THE CUSTOMER

Depending on the business you want to launch, you may be able to try out a competitor's service or product – as a customer. How is their customer service? Are they fast? Cheap? Healthy? You won't find a better way of researching the competition than doing it first hand.

CONCLUSIONS

Once you've gathered all the information you can, make a decision. Do you think your business has enough people saying they will use it (and pay a reasonable price for it) to go ahead? Does anything from the research make you want to change any part of your original idea? You will always learn something useful from market research.

WHAT SORT OF COMPANY SHALL I START?

There are three types of company:

1. Limited company

2. Partnership

3. Sole trader

There are advantages and disadvantages to each type of business, but we think that sole trader is the best way to start your first business. Sole trader — like the name suggests — means that one person is the owner of the company and has complete control over it.

WHY IS IT GOOD FOR ME?

A sole trader company:

* suits small businesses with few or no employees

* means you don't need to open a separate business bank account. You can keep your normal account (but remember to keep careful records on what money is going in and out of your business)

* is a great way to test the market. If you grow, you can always change your business status at a later date.

* Over 70 per cent of UK businesses are sole traders — that's more than 2.3 million businesses — so you're in good company.

WHAT SHOULD I CALL MYSELF?

We'll talk more about choosing the right name for your company in the next chapter. Here we'll deal with the legal side of naming your company. If you want to call your company Ace Computer Repairs, instead of Jack Jones Computer Repairs, for example, you will need to send out invoices (bills for your services) with the company's name and address on them. You can do this at home, and have some fun creating a cool company logo.

If you're a sole trader, you don't legally have to register your company name, but we recommend it. Visit the National Business Register on www.start.biz to get started. You also still need to follow certain rules.

YOUR NAME CAN'T:

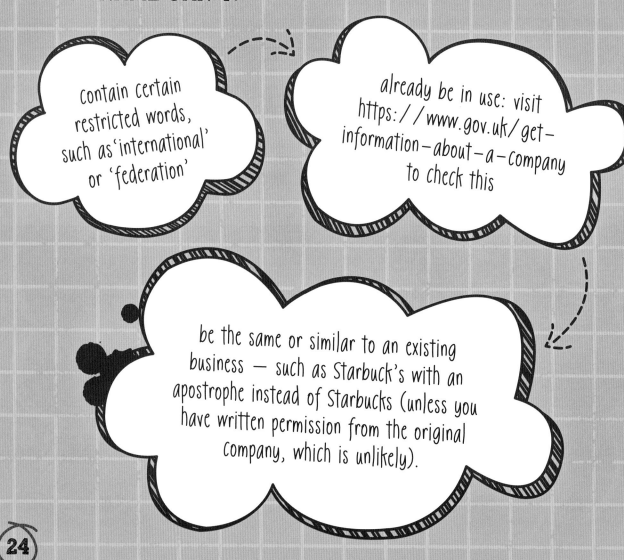

contain certain restricted words, such as 'international' or 'federation'

already be in use: visit https://www.gov.uk/get-information-about-a-company to check this

be the same or similar to an existing business — such as Starbuck's with an apostrophe instead of Starbucks (unless you have written permission from the original company, which is unlikely).

WHAT ELSE DO I NEED TO KNOW?

Check with your local council if you need a licence to operate your business (it varies depending on what kind of business you're planning to run). There are also certain laws that apply to all businesses — big or small.

THE TRADE DESCRIPTIONS ACT

It's actually illegal to make false or misleading claims abut your product or services. So you can't say you're making gluten-free cakes if you're not using gluten-free ingredients.

THE SALE OF GOODS ACT

This states that the goods, i.e. products you sell, must be good quality, be as described, and match your promise about them. Gold-plated handmade bracelets, for example, have a few claims that may need to be proved!

I don't remember it having so many moving parts...

THE SUPPLY OF GOODS AND SERVICES ACT

This says that you have to carry out the service you are advertising with reasonable time, care, skill and cost. If you're going to help people set up and use a home Wi-Fi network, you will need to actually be able to do it, and be available afterwards if it stops working.

WRITING A BUSINESS PLAN

The next step in creating your business is to write a business plan. Don't worry, this isn't going to take weeks and can even be fun. It will definitely help you in the long run — in fact many experts believe that the thought and effort you put into writing a plan is just as important as what's in it! And here are the reasons why:

1 IT WILL HELP YOU DECIDE IF YOUR BUSINESS CAN SUCCEED

If you've properly researched your business, you should now know where your income will be earned. Is there enough to make your business a success? Better to know now than in a year's time!

2 IT WILL ORGANISE YOUR IDEAS

Where's that market research you did last week? What was the name of that supplier you spoke to on the phone? A business plan will put all the necessary information in one place so you can keep referring back to it.

3 IT WILL CREATE A FOCUS

At the start of a new business, there are so many things to do that it's hard to focus on everything, and prioritise some things over others. A business plan will help you:

* set priorities
* establish goals
* measure performance
* answer some key questions like 'Will customers buy our product and how much will they pay?'

4 IT WILL HELP YOU PLAN FOR GROWTH

What will your business look like in 6 months'/2 years'/5 years' time? That might seem like a long way off, but if you can think about it when you start, it will give you and your business some direction in the months and years to come.

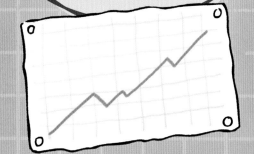

CONTENTS

List your main sections and number pages so that anyone else reading it can find what they are looking for easily. **Tip: do this part last**.

SUMMARY

This is your business in a nutshell:

1. Business name and address.

2. What you do. For example, 'I provide iCloud setup and ongoing technical support for smartphone users', or 'I help local businesses interact with customers through social media.'

3. Your target market, for example 'People without the technical knowledge or confidence to do it for themselves', and where you think your competition will come from. What makes your business different from the competition and why will it stand out?

THE MARKET

How much do you know about the market? Put some time into researching the size, trends, and growth of similar products. Looking at the market in detail will help you get a better understanding of your customers and possible sales, so you can start make plans to increase your business.

YOUR BUSINESS IN DETAIL

Here's where you explain what your business does. Be very specific here: rather than saying 'I want to fix people's computers', you would say something like 'I want to offer technical support to home PC users, focusing on virus removal and prevention, and making sure printers and scanners are working properly'. Will you work on computers in your own home? If so, how will you collect them from customers? **Tip: keep it simple.** If you don't have access to a car, focus on 'on site' repairs. Problem solving is an important part of being an entrepreneur!

YOUNG ENTREPRENEUR: PROPERTY PORTFOLIO

Florida-born teen Willow Tufano helped her estate-agent mum by clearing empty houses and selling the contents on US website Craigslist. Willow then suggested to her mum that they bought a property together and rent it out. Within a year, they had earned their money back and bought a second property. https://www.youtube.com/watch?v=GTTcZC27fko

YOUR EXPERIENCE

For bigger companies, this part of the business plan would cover the company structure – who owns the company, who does what, how qualified everyone is to do their jobs. In your case, your company is likely to have one boss and one employee – you! So write down your own experience and qualifications. Don't worry if you think there's not much to write here – enthusiasm is just as important as experience. And realising there are lots of things you don't know will (hopefully) make you go and do some research.

MARKETING PLANS

This is a **very** important section of the plan. Marketing generates customers, and they mean sales! What kind of customers are you looking for and how will you attract them? You could put leaflets through neighbours' doors, post notices in local shops or online or offer a referral scheme (for example, 'Introduce a friend and get £10 off!'). Look at what your competitors are doing and 'borrow' ideas from them. This part of your business plan should be regularly updated.

WHAT'S YOUR USP?

What makes your business different and, just as importantly, better than what is already out there? Look beyond the product or service that you are offering, and try to come up with some reasons why your business could be better than the others. Could it be the time you take? The price you charge? Free customer support?

SALES TARGETS

Your marketing plan goes hand in hand with your sales targets. If you attract new customers, you'll make sales! So how many sales do you think you can make in the first month? The first year? Be realistic – it will take time for your business to grow.

FINANCIAL FORECAST

Numbers can scare a few people, but don't ignore this part – it's important. Will there be any costs to your business? If you are making something – from cookies to cards or jewellery – there will be a cost to buy the ingredients or materials. There might also be a cost to deliver them. On top of this, you need to put in a cost for your own time (people often try and work out an hourly rate for themselves, based on how long they think it will take to complete one job). From this information, you can produce something called a Profit and Loss, or P&L, forecast.

PUT SIMPLY:

Money (that you have made from sales) — **Costs** (things you have had to buy or money you have had to spend) = **Profit** (or Loss).

If you're selling handmade greetings cards for £2 and they cost you £2.20 to make, you'll need to increase the price, or you make a loss of 20p per card.

MISSION STATEMENT

The final part of your business plan — and definitely one of the most important — is your mission statement. This explains your business in 30 seconds or less. It's sometimes called an 'elevator pitch' because you could explain it to someone on a swift elevator ride. You need to be short, sharp and to the point. Sound tricky? Start by asking yourself the following questions:

✳ why are you in business

✳ who are your customers

✳ what kind of product or service do you provide

✳ what level of service do you offer

✳ what makes you different from your competitors

✳ what image of the business do you want to put across?

Good morning, sir! I'd like to tell you about...

PUTTING IT TOGETHER

Creating a good mission statement will take time, thought and planning, but the effort is worth it. Going through the process should make clear what you're doing and why. Here are a few tips:

2 SPEND TIME ON IT

Mission statements can be as short as one sentence, but writing a good one will take time. Remember, you're searching for language that sums up your business and inspires you.

1 ASK ADVICE

You might be running the business alone, but you can still ask friends and family for their input. They might be able to point out some strengths — and weaknesses — that you've missed.

3 BRAINSTORM

Start with an open mind. Have a few mission statements from other companies to start the discussion. Ask everyone to write down their mission statements for your business, pick the best bits and fit them together.

4 BE INSPIRED AND INSPIRING

Every word counts. Your statement should be dynamic and inspire action. Use interesting, colourful words that you wouldn't use every day — 'sizzle', 'outrageous', 'earth-shattering'. Be bold!

5 START SPREADING THE WORD

Once it's finished, tell people about it. Print it out and stick it on the wall above your computer. Use it on the leaflets you put through letterboxes. Be proud!

GOOD MISSION STATEMENTS

To help people and businesses throughout the world realise their full potential.
Microsoft

We build Gr-r-reat brands and make the world a little happier by bringing our best to you.
Kellogg's

WHIZZ BIZ QUIZ

1. How would you research a business online? Write down five ways you can find out about a business and its customers.

2. What are the advantages of setting up your business as a sole trader?

3. List five good reasons why you should write a business plan before starting your business.

4. Write down the sections that need to be included in a business plan.

5. Find three great company mission statements from existing businesses. What makes them so good?

CHAPTER 3:
MAKING A LASTING IMPRESSION

"Even if you get lucky with something, it's down to you to take the next step and make sure your luck continues."

Nick D'Aloisio (creator of Summly app)

NAMING YOUR BUSINESS

Finding a name for your business is easy, right? Wrong! The right name could be your key to success. The wrong one could be the first step on the road to failure. Some experts suggest an abstract name like Apple — if your customers don't know what to expect from your name, you can create a unique image. Others say names should explain what the business does, like the business social media site LinkedIn.

DOs AND DON'Ts

TIPS TO GET YOU STARTED:

 DO

Think about what message you want to get across. To do this, you'll need to really understand what your business is and what makes it unique. To be effective, the name should reinforce the most important parts of your business. Are you focusing on innovation? Customer service? Technology? The more information your business name communicates to customers, the less time and effort you'll need to spend explaining it!

 DON'T

Ask every single one of your friends and family to help. Why? First of all, you can only choose one name, so everyone whose name wasn't chosen might feel ignored and upset.

DO

Flick through dictionaries (English and foreign), books and magazines to generate ideas.

DON'T

Be boring. The first company in a given market can get away with this — Internet Explorer is a good example — but everyone who comes after needs to be more inventive. That's why Google dreamt up the far more shiny Google Chrome.

DO

Study the competition. The main job of your company name is to set you apart from businesses similar to yours. Look at the companies who are out there already and how they present themselves to decide where you can fit in. If your name is too similar to something a competitor is using, ditch it and try again.

DON'T

Think too small. By this we mean, don't use the name of your street, town or county as part of your company name. It might be fine at the beginning, but could cause confusion with customers when you start to expand.

DON'T

Dream up such a weird name that no one knows what your business does! This is a tricky one: a name with a special meaning can give you a reason to explain your company message to people. For example, Acer, the computer company, means 'sharp' in Latin. But remember your audience: will they understand or remember your company name if it's too obscure? Probably not!

DO

Just choose one or two people whose opinion you really trust. Get them to focus on what your business does, and the type of customers you want to attract.

DON'T

Be a copycat. Frozen yogurt brand Pinkberry inspired lots of imitators who used 'berry' in their name. Better to come up with something strong and simple like Spoon Me (no, we didn't make that up, but it's good right?)

YOUNG ENTREPRENEUR: FISH FLOPS

Maddie Robinson from Texas, USA, decided she wanted to start a business aged just eight! Five years later she launched Fish Flops, a range of children's brightly coloured flip flops, and has more recently expanded into t-shirts, hats and even books! www.fishflops.com

✓ DO

Be flexible. If you pick a name then decide it's not right, be prepared to change it. Learning from your mistakes, and putting them right, is one of the most important things you'll ever learn in business.

✗ DON'T

Name your business after yourself. You may think you've come up with a really good reason to do it — Dick's Dog Walking sounds better than Alan's Dog Walking — but what if you want to expand to looking after other animals? Or pet sitting? It won't be long before you'll need a rebrand!

> Annabelle's Animal Aquarium. Nice!

✓ DO

Sleep on it. If you're lucky, you'll come up with three to five names that you like that pass all your tests. How do you choose the final one? Go back to your original criteria: which name best fits your objectives? Which one best describes your company? Which one do you like best? Read the names aloud, doodle them on a sign or business card. You'll eventually narrow it down to a number one choice.

✗ DON'T

Be afraid to come up with some bad names. You might have to work through a few hundred obvious ideas before you can come up with something brilliant and unique.

✓ DO

Make sure you're legally allowed to use your business name. Hint: no, you can't call yourself Microwsoft Computer Repairs — unless you want a letter in the post from the real Microsoft!

5 GREAT BUSINESS NAMES

1

Samsonite

Named after Samson, who was given supernatural strength by God in the Bible. Far better than the company's original name, The Shwayder Trunk Manufacturing Company!

2

Google

Alternative spelling of the word 'googol' — a number that is 10 to the power of 100. Googol.com wasn't available, but google.com was.

3

Nike

Originally called Blue Ribbons Sports, Nike chose the name of the ancient Greek Winged Goddess of Victory in 1978, and the rest is history.

4

Virgin

Named by its founder Richard Branson because he and his fellow workers were completely new to the world of business.

5

Häagen-Dazs

The name that husband and wife ice-cream makers Reuben and Rose Mattus gave to their company in 1961. It doesn't mean anything, but they liked the sound of it!

STANDING OUT FROM THE CROWD

Who's the young chap in the colourful clothes?

So now you have a name. Congratulations! Your next step is attracting customers, and making your product or service stand out from the competition. In other words, you need to build a brand. Don't worry, it's not as scary as it sounds. We're here to talk you through every step of the way!

WHAT IS A BRAND?

Two hundred years ago, US farmers used to 'brand' the symbol of their ranch on to cattle to show which were theirs when they reached the slaughterhouse. Fast forward 50 years, and the Coca-Cola company started putting its name and logo on to bottles to make it look different from the hundreds of other soda manufacturers on the market.

More recently, marketeers — people who help companies sell more than their competitors — described a brand as 'the intangible sum of a product's attributes'. To you and I, that means 'everything that comes into your head when you think of a certain product'.

Try it. Pick two or three of your favourite brands — from trainers to breakfast cereal — and write down a list of words that you associate with the product or company. It might be 'tasty', 'sporty', 'healthy', 'well made' or any one of a hundred others. When you've finished, you'll see that what you think of a brand is usually a mixture of fact and emotion.

YOUR BRAND—BUILDING CHECKLIST

KNOW YOUR MISSION

Think about the following questions:

✳ why did you start the business

✳ what goals do you want to achieve

✳ what makes your company different?

DECIDE HOW YOU WANT TO BE SEEN

Do you want your brand to be smart and cutting edge? Reliable and trustworthy? Nostalgic? Adventurous? Whatever you want, it won't happen by accident.

THINK LIKE A CUSTOMER

Why do you buy a particular brand? Use the answer to help figure out how your own brand will come across to customers. Use the name, the website, the Facebook page, even the colour of the logo to create the impression you want for your brand.

BE MEMORABLE

Remember the mission statement you created earlier? Try and come up with a catchphrase or slogan that will help people remember your brand. Every time you write or even speak about your business, your language should reflect your brand's values.

DELIVER A GREAT PRODUCT EVERY TIME

You won't build a strong brand if your product or service is unreliable — good one minute, average the next. Consistency — delivering great products or service time after time — is hard to achieve, but it's essential to building a brand. That goes as much for £1 cupcakes as £200 computer repairs.

CHECKLIST

6 WAYS TO BUILD A GREAT BRAND!

1 MAKE YOUR CUSTOMERS FEEL PART OF A TEAM

Try to make your customers feel special and part of a group. If you're offering to set up smartphones, why not start a Facebook page that gives ongoing advice and allows customers to share experiences. Get it right, and you'll build a group of loyal customers.

I'm introducing 'team t-shirts' for every happy customer!

2 CREATE A CHEMICAL REACTION

Experts claim that a chemical called *oxytocin* is released in the brain when we personally interact with people. Oxytocin sparks emotions and memories — exactly what you want for your customers! You could pick up the phone and ask customers if they like your product, or arrange a get-together for customers to share experiences.

YOUNG ENTREPRENEUR: LIZZIE MARIE CUISINE

US teen chef Lizzie Likness started selling healthy home—baked goodies at a local farmer's market at the age of six to pay for horse riding lessons. She launched her food blog at just eight years old and has since been featured on the Huffington Post, CNN and Fox News. www.lizziemariecuisine.com

3 REWARD LOYAL CUSTOMERS

Lots of businesses offer reward schemes — buy five cups of tea and the next one is free! Could you do something similar? Or, even better, follow your most active customers on Twitter (see Point 1) and offer them freebies or loyalty bonuses. It depends on your business, but it could be a free review of their home Wi-Fi service and speed, with advice on how to improve it.

4 USE PEOPLE'S NAMES

As much as possible, make your business about personal service. Try to learn every customer's name and use it whenever you contact them. Even if you're sending out a newsletter, it's easier than ever these days to personalise 'mailouts' with your customers' names. Famous marketeer Dale Carnegie once said, 'The sweetest sound in any language is one's name'. Remember that!

5 DON'T STAND STILL

The best brands are always growing and evolving — that's what keeps them relevant and at the top of their game. When you see a company rebranding — changing its name, or the colour or style of its logo — it's usually because it has failed to move with the times and been left behind. A brand is like a plant — if you don't water it with attention and thought, it will go brown and shrivel up!

6 HAVE A ROLE MODEL

Think of a company whose brand you love. You're not going to copy what they do (they might be in a completely different area of business to you), but you can take inspiration from them. Do they have great adverts? Excellent customer care? An amazing website? Which brings us on to…

GOING ONLINE

NINE TIPS FOR CHOOSING A DOMAIN NAME:

Exciting things can happen online. Vloggers like Zoella and Tanya Burr have built **huge** followings, and even expanded into bestselling books and make-up lines. So even if you plan to offer a traditional product or service, it's important that you don't ignore the Internet.

There are hundreds of books about building a website (we recommend *Quick Expert's Guide: Building A Website*) so we're going to focus on choosing your domain name, and registering it.

1 MAKE IT EASY TO TYPE

If you use slang like 'u' instead of 'you', or alternative spellings like 'xpress' instead of 'express' it can make it harder for customers to find you online.

2 KEEP IT SHORT

If your domain name's long and complicated, there's more chance of your potential customers mistyping or misspelling it.

3 USE KEYWORDS

If you're planning a web design service, try and include the words 'web design' in your URL. It will help improve your rank on search engines and it makes more sense, as you're using the words that people will be searching for online.

4 AVOID NUMBERS AND HYPHENS

You might think www.High5Solutions.com is a great name, but people won't always know if you're using a numeral (5) or a word (five). The same goes for hyphens. Sometimes, it's worth registering different variations for the people who type it incorrectly!

5 BE MEMORABLE

There are millions of domain names out there, so try as hard as you can to make yours stand out! Once you've thought of a name, share it with friends and get their feedback. Does it make sense? Is it easy to remember?

6 RESEARCH IT

Make sure your name isn't already trademarked, copyrighted, or being used by another company. This could save you time and money right at the start.

7 PROTECT YOUR BRAND

If you can afford it, consider buying a few domain extensions (like .co.uk and .biz, as well as .com). This will put off other companies from starting with practically the same name as you, which could confuse customers.

8 ACT QUICKLY

Domain names aren't expensive, so buy one sooner rather than later. You don't want to work on your business for a year, and then find out that all the good domain names are already taken!

9 REGISTER YOUR DOMAIN NAME

Use an Internet service provider (ISP) such as godaddy.com, 123-reg.co.uk or hundreds of others. For around £10 per year, the ISP will do everything needed behind the scenes to make sure your domain is 'live' within a couple of days.

USE THE RIGHT EXTENSION

.Com is the world's most popular end for web addresses, but there are other alternatives:

.co — usually used as a shortcut for company, commerce or community

.info — used for informational sites

.net — mainly used for technical sites

.biz — again, used for business or commercial sites

.me — often used for blogs or personal sites.

CHAPTER 4: SPREADING THE WORD

"Get involved with any business-led school projects... It's not just a novelty school activity. It's business. It's research and networking."

— Nina Devani (creator of Prompt Me Nina password protection app)

You've written a business plan, named your business, and even registered a domain name. Thousands of businesses every year never make it this far, so give yourself a pat on the back. But what's next? You need to let customers know about your business. It's called 'marketing' and here's how to be great at it!

THE BASICS OF MARKETING

RESEARCH

Find out what your customers really want — is it cheaper prices, home delivery? Feedback from customers is invaluable, and this builds on the research you have already done for your business plan. *https://www.surveymonkey.com* is a good place to start for creating questionnaires.

TARGET MARKET

Do you know who your target market is? In other words, the group of customers (based on age, geographical area and interests) that you're aiming your business towards.

TRY THIS TEST

* give your ideal customer an age (within a 10-year range)

* are they male or female

* what do they do

* where do they go

* what interests them?

Building a picture of your customer will help you connect with him or her through your marketing campaigns.

COMPETITION

Look at what your competitors are doing and try to work out how to a) steal market share and b) use any failings to your advantage. It's important to look at relevant competitors, though — if you're making homemade ice cream, don't say that Ben and Jerry's is your competitor.

USP

Aim to be truly unique. Good customer service and business knowledge are essentials to your business, not USPs. **'Understand and work your SMART TV remote in 30 minutes or your money back'** is a great USP!

Let's hope bees never go out of fashion...

CONSISTENCY

Experts say your brand is the promise you make to your customer. If you change a logo, or company colours, or start offering guitar lessons as well as computer repairs, you're saying to customers that you're not certain you're doing the right thing.

13 WAYS TO MARKET YOUR BUSINESS ON NEXT TO NO BUDGET

1 WRITE A PRESS RELEASE

This should explain what your business does and how it's unique. Send it to local newspapers and radio stations, drop it into local leisure centres and health clubs. All of these are free of charge. Include your company's web address or Facebook page so interested customers can find you!

2 SET UP A FACEBOOK PAGE FOR YOUR BUSINESS

Update your status regularly to let your customers know what you're up to. (Be sure to make it business–related, not how you're getting on with FIFA.) People need to be aware of your business to be able to use it. Ask for feedback from previous customers and suggestions for additional services you could offer. If you're making organic cookies, post photos of your latest batch coming out of the oven looking mouth–watering.

3 SET UP A WEBSITE

A good website is essential. If a customer is looking for anything from computer repairs to dog walking, they'll Google it. A great-looking website will make your business appear professional and help it grow.

4 START A BLOG

An informative blog will increase traffic to your website. You can offer advice about what you do that people will find useful. If they like your posts, they'll be more likely to use your business.

YOUNG ENTREPRENEUR: ZACK'S WEB DESIGNS

Zack Weisenthal caught the web design bug at 14. He attended a class about WordPress (a web design tool) and was inspired to create his own site. He quickly branched out and built sites for lots of companies, from charities to racing car drivers. www.zackswebdesigns.com

5 USE YOUR CUSTOMERS TO PROMOTE YOUR BUSINESS

Potential customers are far more likely to use a business that's been recommended by a friend, so offer discounts to customers if someone they recommended buys something. Loyal customers saying great things about you is the best marketing.

6 OFFER A LOYALTY DISCOUNT CARD

This is a great way to reward customers for their loyalty, and persuade them to keep coming back. '**Buy three homemade candles, and get the fourth free**'. Major companies like Starbucks use this, and it works.

7 SPREAD THE WORDS OF HAPPY CUSTOMERS

Ask customers to write a short email about the positive experience they had using your business. Put these 'testimonials' on your website and blog. People will be more likely to use your business if they see that other customers have had a positive experience.

8 RUN A COMPETITION

Giving something away can get new people talking about your business. Watch how often big companies do this. You might not be able to offer free holidays, but you can offer free PC repairs for a month, or a free birthday cake for a party. Any prize you give away is an opportunity to show a new customer how great your business is!

9 MAKE A GREAT BUSINESS CARD

Business cards are cheap and a great way of helping people to remember your business – even if you're an online business! So take some time to come up with a design that people won't forget. Whenever you meet a potential customer, give them a business card. If it's really great, they might even show it to their friends. It's worth remembering too, to 'brand' all your social media accounts, Twitter, Facebook and so on, with the company name and – if appropriate – web address, so they can all act as 'online business cards' for you.

10 TRY TO WIN AN AWARD

Investigate what awards are available in your industry. It could even be a local '**Young Entrepreneur of the Year**'. Enter as many of these as you can. If you win, it's a great story for the local press who'll definitely want to write about it. You can mention it on your website, blog and even include it on a business card ... which you're going to make next.

YOUNG ENTREPRENEUR OF THE YEAR AWARD!

Hope I get a mention in the acceptance speech.

WHIZZ BIZ QUIZ

1. Can you name the five basics of marketing?

2. List 10 ways you can market your business on next to no budget.

3. What does USP stand for?

4. What does it mean?

5. Think of competitions your business could run to promote itself.

11 ASK A BLOGGER

Is there a blogger in your field who you really admire? If so, why not try to get them to write about your business and put it on your website. Regularly updating your site will help it climb the Google rankings, and guest posts attract new visitors.

12 START A YOUTUBE PAGE

Whatever your business, you'll have great specialist knowledge of what you do. So why not start making short, informative 'How To' videos on YouTube? It can show customers that you really know what you're talking about.

YOUNG ENTREPRENEUR: MANSCANS

Hart Main launched his 'candles for men' business in 2011 when he was just 13, with smells including 'Bacon' and 'Sawdust'. His company buys tins of soup, donates them to homeless shelters, then collects the empty cans to use as candle holders. So far, Hart's business has donated over 100,000 meals to hungry people. www.man−cans.com

13 HELP OUT A LOCAL CHARITY

Organising a fundraising event, or giving 5 per cent of earnings from a campaign to a local charity, can help your local community and get you coverage in the local press.

CHAPTER 5: UNDERSTANDING FINANCES

"I'm not an A+ student ... [but] having this business ... has given me more confidence in school."

Noa Mintz (NanniesByNoa.com)

Now we're going to talk about money. Making it using a sales plan, collecting it through invoicing and credit control, and managing it with simple bookkeeping.

WRITE A SALES PLAN

A sales plan simply explains how you will grow your business – this is usually through a mixture of a) finding new customers, and b) doing more business with existing customers. Simple really! So how do you do it?

Decide what specific and unique benefits your business provides. You may save people time, increase their knowledge, or improve their health. In other words, what customer needs are you meeting?

A GOOD EXAMPLE:

'Ace Smartphones offers fast, affordable smartphone set-up and ongoing technical advice for all smartphones and budgets. We now offer 'phone-a-friend' deals, which give customers 20 per cent discount on future visits if they introduce a friend to us.'

WORK OUT YOUR POSITION IN THE MARKET

You might be offering a clever or unique solution to a common problem, or providing a service that's more affordable or easier to access for a local market. For example, customers might find it cheaper and less intimidating to have you set up their new smartphone than take it to a high street shop, or try to do it themselves.

CAREFULLY SET YOUR PRICES

Research similar products or services and set your prices carefully. Make them low enough to be competitive — so customers choose you over a similar business — but high enough to make a profit. Also think longer term, about how you can increase prices and customer spending by offering additional services.

SET YOUR SHORT— AND LONG—TERM REVENUE GOALS

Plan how much money you hope to make in, say, six months and two years. Be realistic. Think about how much time you can spend on the business if you have exams, for example. Don't just make numbers up: base your figures on existing income and how (hopefully) it has grown since you first started. And try to imagine what changes may occur in your market, and how that will affect your revenue goals. For example, smartphone ownership is increasing so your number of potential customers for your technical support is also increasing.

CONSIDER PLANS TO EXPAND

Is it possible to expand the area, and therefore potential customer base, that you sell to? If you find new customers two, three, five miles from where you live, how would you get there? Is it worth your time, based on what you are currently charging? Could you even charge extra for your travel?

ADVERTISE YOUR BUSINESS

How will you let new customers know about your business? It could be a website, leaflets through doors, a Facebook or Twitter account or something else. When you contact a business, they will often ask 'How did you hear about us?' That's because they are trying to work out which methods of advertising are getting the best results. Do the same thing, and see how it works for you!

PLAN YOUR SALES STRATEGY

Be specific: will you be producing 100 leaflets to deliver through letterboxes? Writing a press release (see page 44) to send to 10 radio stations and three local papers? Give yourself targets, as they are easier to measure. Plus you'll feel great when you break them!

GETTING PAID

You've worked hard, created your business, and you're starting to attract customers. Now we're going to talk about collecting money! Depending on what kind of business you run, you may get paid immediately for your work, or you might have to wait days, sometimes weeks, for your money. Here are some examples:

PAID STRAIGHT AWAY	PAID LATER
✳ dog walking	✳ web design
✳ selling gifts (direct to customers)	✳ selling gifts (to shops)
✳ tuition	✳ youTuber
✳ smartphone set-up.	✳ building an app.

If you're getting paid later for your work, credit control is important. This is how businesses keep track of what they are owed, so they remember to chase payment.

You'll need to start producing invoices for work you've done. An invoice is basically a 'notice' you send to customers letting them know that payment is due.

CREATING YOUR INVOICE

Like everything to do with business, an invoice might seem complicated, but actually it's very easy. Just remember to include the following information on it:

We've included a sample invoice over the page to give you a better idea.

✳ your company name

✳ your company address

✳ name and address of the person you're sending the invoice to

✳ the date you sent the invoice

✳ a unique reference number so you can keep track of all your individual invoices

✳ a short description of the service or product you provided

✳ details of how to pay the invoice, e.g. either by cheque to your company name (unlikely but some older customers might prefer to pay this way), or more likely with your bank account details so it can be paid electronically by bank transfer

✳ don't forget to include payment terms, too — that's the amount of time you'll allow the customer to take before they pay the invoice. This can vary between 7–30 days. Try and keep the time period as short as possible!

SOME OTHER IMPORTANT POINTS TO REMEMBER:

✳ send the invoice as soon as the job is done or the product delivered

✳ keep copies of your invoices carefully filed either on a computer or in a folder, under Paid and Unpaid

✳ make a timetable for chasing payments — start with the oldest ones first!

Ace Smartphones

225 High Street
Anytown
Herts
TD23 5RT

INVOICE

Date: ....

Invoice number: ....

Customer's name: ....

Address: ....

Email: ....

Job description:

....

....

....

....

Please make cheques payable to
'Ace Smartphones' or bank transfer to

Ace Smartphones

Account number 12345678

Sort code 12-34-56   **Payment terms:** 14 days

Thank you for choosing Ace Smartphones.

BALANCING THE BOOKS

Bookkeeping is just another word for managing your money. If you're a sole trader, your bookkeeping should be simple. Remember to keep receipts for everything you buy or spend money on to run your business — these are your costs. And keep copies of all the invoices you make for the work you do — this is your income.

Profit equals income minus costs.

We recommend managing your accounts on a computer. All you need is a simple spreadsheet. Break the business down by month and have one column for income and another for costs. It's important to keep this up to date. Also, keeping a record here of when invoices were sent out and paid (or not paid) will help with your credit control.

WHIZZ BIZ QUIZ

1. Explain what a sales plan does and why it's important.

2. Explain how you would set your prices.

3. List five businesses where you would get paid straight away, and five where you would have to wait to be paid.

4. Write down all the information that you need to include on an invoice.

5. What is profit?

YOUNG ENTREPRENEUR: GLADIATOR LACROSSE

Florida-born Rachel Zietz loved lacrosse, but found it hard to afford the equipment. With the help of a young entrepreneur group, the 13-year-old created a range of quality, affordable equipment. In three years, the company made £700,000 in revenue, and Rachel was shortlisted for a Young Entrepreneur award! www.gladiatorlacrosse.com

CHAPTER 6: GROWING YOUR BUSINESS

"Follow your dreams. If you put your mind to it, you can accomplish anything...
Just believe in yourself."

Alina Morse (creator of Zollipops)

MAKING THE MOST OF YOUR TIME

Your business is doing well and you're busy. Great! Or is it? Sometimes it feels like there's just too much to do, and not enough time to do it in. That's why you need our top tips for managing your time.

Ooh, I feel queasy!

Perhaps we shouldn't have sold him those five cupcakes...

SET GOALS

One of the things we hope you've learned from reading this book is the importance of planning. And that goes for time management too. Setting yourself goals will not only give you something to focus on, but it will also help you work out what is and isn't worth spending your time on. **Tip: Start by asking yourself where you want to be in six months' time** (no we don't mean Thorpe Park), but make sure your goals are realistic and achievable. Selling your computer repair business to Sir Alan Sugar in 12 months may be a little over-ambitious!

Here are some ideas:

* within six months of launching, I want to be adding 10 new customers to the business every month

* within a year, I want to be in the top three businesses of my kind in my local area

* in year two, I want to double turnover from year one.

YOUNG ENTREPRENEUR: MO'S BOWS

Bowtie-loving Moziah Bridges, from Memphis, USA, started Mo's Bows when he was just nine years old! Well-dressed Mo designs and sells his range of ties through his own website and in stores. Next step for Mo? A full clothing range! www.mosbowsmemphis.com

PRIORITISE

It's difficult to know which tasks to tackle first. Our advice: do the most important things first. Sounds simple, right? But how do you know? Ask yourself three questions:

why am I doing this task

how does this task help me achieve my goals

to what extent does this task help me achieve my goals?

KEEP A TO-DO LIST

Do you have trouble remembering everything you need to do? Find yourself forgetting important jobs?

A to-do list is a reminder of what you need to do, and when. It helps break things down into small, manageable tasks or steps. Write down what you need to do in order of importance — from 'Very' to 'Not very'. Try highlighting urgent tasks so they jump off the page. And enjoy crossing things off as you do them!

FOCUS ON ONE THING AT A TIME

Multitasking sounds impressive, but it doesn't work. Business researchers say multitasking takes up 20–40 per cent more time. They recommend focusing on one task at a time.

AVOID DISTRACTIONS

Receiving email alerts, texts and social media messages stops you from using your time effectively. They can distract you, lower your productivity, cause stress and can stop you from finishing important tasks on time. Work out what's your most common distraction and stop it. That means switching off your phone or email alerts until you've finished the job. The positive feeling you get from taking control of your time will be worth it!

CUSTOMER SERVICE

When you're busy, it's also important to ensure that the product or service you're providing is as good as it can possibly be every time. To build a great company, and ultimately a great brand, you have to give 100 per cent and deliver great results time after time. So here are three questions to ask yourself the next time a job comes in.

1 CAN I GET IT DONE IN TIME?

Every customer you deal with has an expectation of when they want a job done by. So be honest with yourself and them. Don't think you'll be able to fix their PC for another week? Can't get round to walk their dog until 4.30 pm? Tell them. You might lose some work, but you'll keep your reputation. Take on a job and don't deliver on what you promised, and you and your business will have a black mark against you. With luck, a customer may respect your honesty and be more flexible, so you can still do their job. That's a win-win!

2 AM I CHARGING ENOUGH?

You need to consider how much you should charge for your time, let's say by the hour and by the day. It's common for new business owners to underestimate how long something will take to complete, and not charge enough. Don't be afraid to ask questions so you fully understand the job. Experience will help with this, but our advice is to always assume it will take longer than you first expect. If you charge that little bit more, it will stop you from rushing to finish the job, and make sure your quality stays high.

3 HOW DO I NEGOTIATE?

Making money is an important part of your business. So what happens when a customer asks, 'How much do you charge?' If you really don't know what to charge, our tip is to throw the question back and ask a) do they have a budget in mind, and b) how long do they expect the job to take. Give the impression that you're flexible (not that you don't know!). If you feel awkward doing this face to face, send your new clients an estimate by email. This will give you time to think, and avoid confusion because the figures are recorded.

YOUNG ENTREPRENEUR: EDGE

British school friends Ed Hardy and Kit Logan launched skiing app Edge, aged just 17. The app, which is free to download and funded by advertising, can track skiers' perfomances, and reviews favourite mountainside restaurants and bars. The pair have won the support of experienced tech investors, including the team behind music app Spotify. www.edgemobile.co/

STAYING MOTIVATED

However enjoyable your business is, we understand that there will be times when you wish you could just play Playstation/watch 'Made In Chelsea'/put your headphones in and listen to your favourite band* (*possibly all three). So we're going to leave you with our four top tips on staying motivated.

1 TIDY YOUR DESK

Take 10 minutes now and file everything away in the right place. Clean your computer screen and desk. Ahhh, doesn't that feel better?

2 CHECK YOUR GOALS

Remember the goals you set in our Time Management section (see page 55)? Check back on them and monitor your progress. Do this once a week. If you spot that you're falling behind, you can get back on track.

3 READ SOMETHING INTERESTING

Articles and books from famous entrepreneurs can really motivate you to follow in their footsteps. But that's not the only way to put a spring in your step.

If you're a football fan, watching YouTube videos of great goals would get you buzzing. Or maybe a song from your favourite band? Find out what works best for you.

4 REWARD YOURSELF

What do you really like? Whether it's new trainers, or a Hawaiian pizza, treat yourself from time to time as a reward for all your hard work. Along the same lines, don't feel guilty if you want to take a few days' break — as long as you haven't got clients waiting for their jobs. You'll come back with a spring in your step and ready to take on the world again.

GLOSSARY

Abstract – relating to an idea or quality rather than a real object or thing

Affiliate marketing – when an online retailer pays an outside website for visitors or sales generated from reviews or recommendations

Banner ad – an advert that runs across the top of a web page

Brainstorm – a group discussion to produce ideas or solve problems

Click-throughs – the number of visitors to a web page who follow a link to get to that site

Configure – arrange or set up a computer system, or part of it

Copyright – the exclusive legal right to print, publish or reproduce something, often music, film or literature

Creativity – the use of imagination or original ideas to create something

Criteria – standards by which something is judged or decided

Dynamic – positive, full of energy and ideas

Engage your audience – entertain and interest a targeted group of people

Entrepreneur – someone who sets up a business, taking on financial risks in the hope of making a profit

Evolving – developing gradually to suit a need

First-hand – from personal experience

Forecast – a prediction or estimation about the future

Generate – produce or create

Guru – an influential teacher or expert

Informative – providing useful or interesting information

Innovation – the introduction of new ideas or products

Inspirational – giving someone the urge to do something, usually creative

Intangible – difficult to define or explain

Intimidating – frightening or worrying (because it seems complicated or difficult)

Invaluable – extremely useful

Mailouts – posting or emailing information about your business or service to lots of people at the same time

Maximise – to make something as large or as great as possible; to make the best use of something

Minimal – very small

Misleading – giving the wrong idea or impression

Monetise – to earn money from something

Nostalgic – creating memories or a feeling of the past

Objectives – goals; aims

Obscure – vague; hard to remember or define

Optimism – hopefulness and confidence about the future or success of something

Potential – possibility

Price point – a position on a scale of possible prices that your product or service could be sold at

Prioritise – put first; judge as being most important

Profit margin – the amount by which the money you make from sales exceeds your costs

Registering – entering a name on to an official list or directory

Reinforce – strengthen or support an existing feeling or idea

Relevant – appropriate to the current time or situation

Strategy – a plan of action designed to achieve a long-term goal

Subscription – an arrangement to receive something regularly, like a webcast, often by paying for it

Testimonial – a statement (usually from a customer) talking about the quality of your product or service

Trademark – a symbol or words legally registered to represent a company or product, for example the Nike swoosh

Tutorial – an explanation of a subject, often step-by-step

INDEX

FURTHER INFORMATION

USEFUL WEBSITES

http://startups.co.uk/young-entrepreneurs/

http://www.forbes.com/sites/jasonma/2015/02/24/twelve-of-todays-most-impressive-young-entrepreneurs/

http://www.huffingtonpost.co.uk/news/young-entrepreneurs/

www.entrepreneur.com

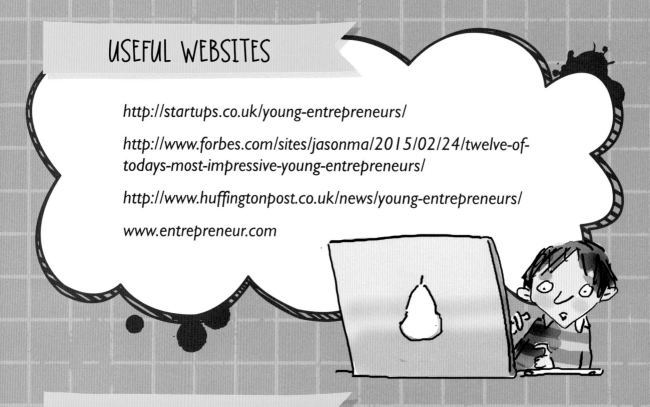

USEFUL BOOKS

Quick Expert's Guide: Building A Website by Chris Martin (WAYLAND, 2012)

Cash, Savings and All That Stuff: A Guide to Money and How to Manage It by Kira Vermond and Clayton Hanmer (FRANKLIN WATTS, 2014)

The Facebook Effect: The Inside Story of the World's Fastest Growing Company by David Kirkpatrick (VIRGIN BOOKS, 2011)

How to Build a Billion Dollar App: Discover the secrets of the most successful entrepreneurs of our time by George Berkowski (PIATKUS, 2014)